HOLES OF OUR YOUTH

By Ken Burger
with Photographs by
David Lissy

TDK Publishing
Charleston, South Carolina

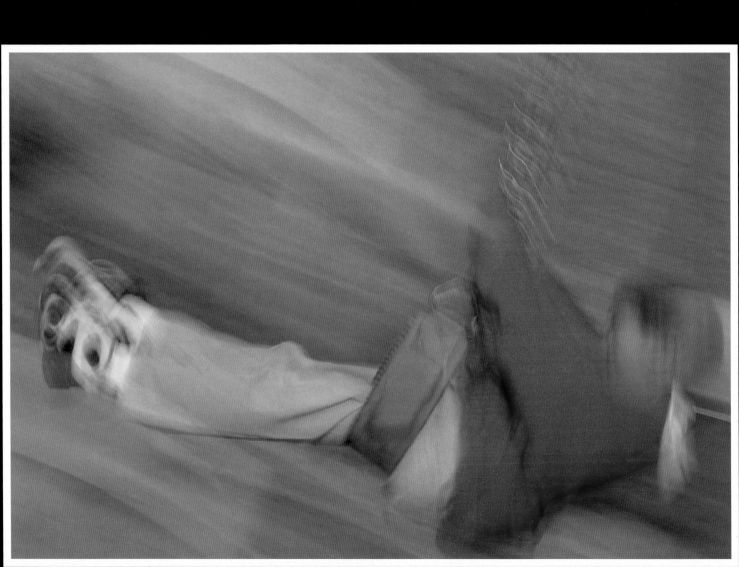

OREWORD

Sports is many things to many people.

For some it is a quarterback dropping back in the pocket, scanning the field and hitting his wide receiver in the end zone for the game-winning touchdown.

But it's also a young man staring helplessly at a math book in a classroom far removed from the playing field and knowing his body is better trained than his mind.

Sports for some is the excitement created when men and women of extraordinary talents compete for enjoyment and praise, finding within themselves the ability to excel on command.

But it's also a young boy crying in the rain behind the bleachers because he's made a child's mistake and didn't live up to the expectations of a father trying to recapture the glories of his youth.

Sports is a point guard weaving his way through a maze of defenders, using finesse and agility to pull up and hit a jump shot at the buzzer to win the championship game.

But it's also a teenager who has learned to answer questions from the media by watching his heroes on television, but when the gym is quiet and the fans have gone home still struggles with the embarrassment of acne and the human questions of self worth.

Sports is the wonderful thrill of anticipation and hype that precedes an event that captures the imagination of a nation and reaches a fever pitch of emotions that is unequalled in the more mundane aspects of our lives.

But it's also the dull thud of disappointment that comes when the gods of our fantasies perform like mortals and suffer the bitter sting of sarcasm from those who previously praised them.

Sports is the sweet smell of freshly-mown grass on a golf course in the early morning, yet undisturbed by the hordes that will come to see men test their skills against the subtle slopes and man-made hazards.

It is also the pungent odors of sweat and blood and ointments and mud and tape and socks and steam and aftershave that clash in a post-game locker room, win or lose.

Sports is a source of pride that swells in our hearts when our children do well or our favorite team climbs to a pinnacle of success recognized by our peers.

But it's also the ugly animosity that too often rages between fans and brings people to blows when they take children's games too seriously.

Sports, as it should be, is a diversion from the realities of life and death and taxes and car payments and mortgages and doctor bills and office politics. It is a competitive cornerstone of our society that gives us joy and laughter and hope for the next season.

In this book, this collection of columns and photographs, may you find whatever it is you think sports means to you.

FOOTBALL

Photos courtesy of the Van Buskirk family

Life Through the Earholes of Our Youth

Most of us have memories of high school football, as vague and distorted as they may be. So as today's youngsters plod out to the sweat-soaked fields where blocking sleds wait like oversized linemen, we tend to fantasize about the time we spent eating and spitting the August grasses of our youth.

We were, of course, much tougher back then. At least in our own minds. Back when football players were measured by an insane ability to go hours without water and bet their health on salt pills that were dry-heaved on the sidelines when coaches weren't looking.

Looking back through the distorted hour glass of time gives us a romantic view of football. We remember things the way we want them remembered. The way we have told our children it was so often that we begin to believe it ourselves

And it's amazing how a black-and -white team picture in an old high school yearbook sometimes hides the painful truth. That maybe we weren't really that good.

Or maybe we didn't play as much as we remember. Or maybe, in some cases, we only lasted long enough to be in the team picture.

Somewhere between the way we see it now and the way others saw it, is the truth. Told or untold.

Mine, however, is not a memory romanticized. Eighth-grade football may have been the most brutal thing I've ever experienced. And not just for me, but for all the boys my age and size who had no business on the field other than proving something to somebody else. And nobody knew it better than the coach, bless his soul.

For he had the eye. He was a man who could see an athlete coming a mile away. There is a walk, a stance, a genetic mechanism that makes a boy at rest look like a man in full stride.

You know it when you see it. And when you don't. There has never been a coach yet who can out-coach chromosomes. Some have tried. All have failed.

Those of us not born to football were not, however, without some sense of courage. The time

and place demanded it. And the alternative was too terrifying to imagine.

So we gave ourselves to the game that would test our tenacity if nothing else. Peer pressure being the motivator. Survival the ultimate goal.

Too small. Too slow.

But also too scared not to be there the day they handed out the gear. And at the end of the line where the small and slow were outfitted with the leftovers of the big and fast.

Shoes that were too big. Broken shoulder pads. No hip pads. Helmets you could spin around on your head.

Football is a tough enough game to figure out at ground level as it is. But watching it through the earholes of your football helmet can make it even tougher.

To the coach's credit, he didn't run us off. He should have, perhaps, and we would have, no doubt.

But we slogged through the calisthenics and blocking drills and wind sprints, tripping over our oversized shoes, our broken equipment flapping in the wind and falling to the ground behind us.

If there was a shortage of blocking dummies, no problem. We were always available to provide resistance. Two or three of us at once, if that's what it took to slow down a promising fullback.

We were, by football standards, expendable. Also perishable, as the coach knew full well. For we were one-season wonders. Notching our young gun-belts with an experience expected and tried.

Failure, after all, was forgivable. Cowardice was not.

So we endured the punishment for the simple satisfaction of being a part of something that was such a big part of our youth. A few quit, but most of us hung on until the end.

And when the season was over and future stars had been identified and promised varsity status, our fate was no less gratifying.

We had done what was expected of us and lived to tell about it. We even had our pictures taken for the yearbook, down on one knee, helmets at our side. And that, in hindsight, may be the best memory of all.

5

Sights & Sounds of Prep Football

There is something about the first night of high school football. There is a certain smell in the air, that mixture of hotdogs and popcorn and new-mown grass and sweat and the unusual aroma of a hundred perfumes when a gaggle of cheerleaders passes by.

And there are the sounds, of pads popping and chants and cheers and scratchy loudspeakers and bands blaring away as young children run and scream in the night because everybody else is and because they can.

If there is something special about the first day of spring and the last day of school and Christmas morning that makes us feel the passing of time, then the first Friday night of the football season has become another calendar that marks our way.

Because high school football is a part of us all. Whether we played it or watched it, we know it's part of what makes us Americans and September would not follow August if we could not smell it and hear it on the wind and know it was going on somewhere as it always has.

And, it seems, it always has. As far back as our grandfathers there has been football. And there will, no doubt, be football when we are grandfathers as well.

Some say football is the same whether you are 14 or 40, but that's not really true.

When you are 14, football is a fun but frightening affair filled with all sorts of possibilities for failure. From fumbled punts to dropped passes to busted plays, the game is fraught with opportunities for a young man to embarrass himself in front of those who he would least like to see him fail.

There are, in case you didn't know, many more mistakes than moments of glory in high school football. They just don't make the highlight films.

The 40-year-olds, meanwhile, have mostly forgotten the fear that follows the opening whistle. They are result-oriented and demanding, too far removed from it all to remember what it was really like. If somebody yelled at them today, for instance, the way a high school coach yells at a high school football player, there would be a fight or a lawsuit or both.

Nobody takes more helpful abuse than football players who have to take it whether they want it or not.

It's long been argued that sports in general, and football in particular, strengthen the American male vertebrae and prepare us for life in the real world.

Maybe it's so. Maybe it's not. If it's true, then what do women have that's the equivalent of football? Cheerleading? Playing piccolo in the band? Are we to conclude that our daughters will never know true success because they've never played football?

Don't they need to build character as well as the boys? Can they not know real success unless they've scored a touchdown, recovered a fumble, or kicked a field goal? Will the pains of their adult lives be tougher because they've never suffered through a losing season, a broken rib, athlete's foot or a bad case of jock itch?

A lot of people don't buy into that anymore, but surely somebody's done a study on it.

Something that shows that 98% of all jet fighter pilots played high school football, without noting that maybe 98% of those who built and designed them did not.

But where else can young men vent their natural aggression and be cheered on by their parents and

young girls in short skirts for doing so?

That's why football is such a great game for the young. Because those who don't have to play it have made it that way.

Whether or not it's the game that's made us great or it's just something we use to mark the end of another summer and the beginning of another school year, if you grew up in America it's part of you.

It's teenage girls chattering endlessly in the stands, cheerleaders cheering to themselves, bands battling with their brass, parents correcting the spelling of their son's name in the program, coaches coaching like every game is the Super Bowl, and players dreaming of heroics amid the madness.

Surrounding it all is a sweet intensity that can only be generated on a Friday night beneath the lights when the wind carries the sounds and smells of football that are like no other.

Friday Nights Just Aren't As Simple Today

When I walked into the stadium and stood quietly, staring across the small sea of faces in the stands, she looked at me with a flash of happy recognition and a tiny wave before re-embracing the strict discipline required of a 15-year-old piccolo player in the high school band.

Knowing she would not be free for a hug and a kiss until after the halftime performance, I took a cold seat high in the stands, out of her line of vision, to wait my turn along with the other segregated and separated of our society.

It was here that I realized that high school football crowds are not always what they appear to be—the Norman Rockwell image of small-town life painted in harmonic strokes.

Instead they can be more like a Van Gogh, sometimes distorted, but always revealing.

Down below, as the young boys played the game and the cheerleaders cheered to themselves and 15-year-old piccolo players strained to be heard over the percussion section, the picture fought itself to find a fuzzy focus.

Beside me sat a man who wore the soft clothes of a house divided, the hard look of a searching soul.

Between fumbles and blocked punts we talked football the way men do, in quick generalities, to establish our knowledge and right to be there.

Psychologists prefer to believe it is our way of avoiding real thought, but it's more than that. It's as standard as a handshake, more telling than a confession.

His discussion gave him away as surely as if he had been strapped to a couch. For out on the field was his son, a skinny defensive end who played with the kind of tenacity and insecurity inherent in high school football.

This man did not have to tell me his life story. I knew instantly. Whenever his boy did well, his rise to applaud was always accompanied by a quick glance to another section of the stands where a woman his

age did the same, both cheering a little louder than those around them.

Behind the facemask, neither could see which, if either, the skinny boy acknowledged or whether he chose to transact his emotional business through the next play.

At halftime my eyes, and others from another section, were riveted on the pretty piccolo player whose long hair was tucked tightly up under a hat, making her look the same as all the other marchers.

But even across a football field, your eyes can always find the walk and stance of your own no matter how much they zig and zag through the maze of other people's children.

And there is no less satisfaction in a perfect left-facing maneuver than there is in a sack for a loss. They are equally awe-inspiring when weighed against the seemingly short span of time since their first steps.

And despite the terrible acoustical cacophony that echoed between the brass, concrete and the black open sky, there was a piccolo peaking just above it all as if privately performed in a concert hall.

When she broke ranks we sat and talked and I tried to tell her the million thoughts I had been meaning to write in letters that never made the mail.

She laughed and said she knew how it was,

sharing her glances with me and a polite young trombonist who stood shyly in the wings.

Too soon she had to return to the formation, striking a pose any military man would admire.

I left before the game ended, walking slowly from the bright lights into the chilled darkness, glancing back as if reprinting a Kodak moment would make it last longer.

High in the stands I saw my soulmate standing to applaud his skinny defensive end. I could not see his eyes, but knew they were still darting from the field to another corner of the stands and back.

From the parking lot I heard the band strike up a fight song similar to one that has risen from all high school games played through the ages.

I remember thinking how simple these events used to be, and how they're not so simple anymore.

Mother Nature Wasn't Told About Football in August

The temperature was in the '90s and the humidity hung like a soggy blanket that could not be kicked off during a bad dream. Sweat ran in rivers of boiling blood and every step seemed like it might be the last.

The cool, crisp nights of autumn were light years away. Heat was the enemy of the moment and would be for months to come.

But we pushed ahead. Not from genuine desire or dedication or love of the game, but from fear. Of not measuring up. Of looking weak in front of our friends. Of failure.

Football was, and forever will be, a passage from childhood to the mystical realm of manhood in America. It has been written. There was no pain we would not endure, no frustration we would not tolerate and no weakness we would not hide. For under the heavy armor, little boys were ceremoniously melted and transformed into men.

That's the way it was, and the way it is.

The first day of football practice is the best day of the rest of the season. It's a day of loud noises and laughter, but little pain. There are drills to be learned, sprints to be run and tests to be taken. But the mind is still lost in echoes of cheers in the distance.

Even the idea of two-a-days cannot diminish the dreams of children who long for glory but do not yet know the price. They can only hear the bands and cheerleaders and hope to make the highlight films of Friday nights to come.

They have not fallen breathless on the sidelines wondering if they can rise and run again. They have not experienced the dizzy daze of losing their place in time and space and wondering where they are. They are still days or weeks away from questioning the sense of this passage.

From the beginning it is a fraternity of fascination. To be uniformed and identified as a member of the team is nothing less than essential in a boy's mind. He will run through fire to feel that oneness with his peers and catch a knowing wink from his father.

But the days will grow hotter and longer. Walls of heat will appear in the mornings and grow

until they seem insurmountable. The air will be heavy with moisture, at times too heavy to breathe.

Bodies will evaporate and legs will burn with aches that mother's massage cannot soothe. One practice will run into the next, and soon the vision of glory shimmers like an unreachable oasis. And there will be no place to hide.

The game that looks like a graceful gazelle in November is a wild untamed demon in August. But they cannot dismount.

To ride is to win. To fall is to fail. They hang on with all they have.

But that may not be enough. Star quarterbacks do not sweat more than third-string tackles. The same sun broils their backs. The same sweat burns their eyes. Practice puts everyone in his place. All the places on earth are hot, and hurt has no discretion.

But there is learning beyond the signals and diagrams of the game. They will learn to appreciate a cloud that moves slowly across the sun and eases the penetrating heat, if only for a moment. They will blow across the field and cool the body and soul. They will taste water for the first time, and never take it for granted again.

They will learn to look to the skies for rain and pray for showers that could cool the day and make mud of the choking dust. And they will re-learn the sleep of a child that serves as escape.

For when day is done, there is no solace in knowing tomorrow may be better. It may not be. And when August turns to September, there is no promise of improvement. For the equinox is unyielding, and the leaves are still quite green.

Mother Nature won't bring her cool winds until the time has come. She will not turn her burning eyes away until she's ready.

Nobody told her about football practice in August.

PORCHLIGHTS

What Happened to the World of Our Fathers?

I remember when my parents used to convert our small living room into three tables for bridge and their friends would arrive after supper, talking the talk of grownups.

From eye level to a cardtable, I remember the women smoking incessantly, their lipstick painted on the cigarette filters, the smoke mixing decadently with their long legs, stockings and high heel shoes.

The men were all tall and gaunt, not far removed from their days in the war, veterans of a victory they never talked about in the company of small boys.

In the early 1950s, small-town America was nothing like the world we live in today. It was self-contained. Heroes lived next door.

Only the rich had television. The wide world of sports existed only as fuzzy photographs in the newspaper.

I don't remember my father being much of a sports fan. If he was, he never made much of it.

In middle age, he took up golf and played on Sunday afternoons after church, a pull-cart trailing behind him as he walked the 9-hole layout that passed for a golf course in our town.

I'm sure there were those who followed the careers of Babe Ruth and Lou Gehrig more closely than I realized, but it was never the talk of the town.

We lived in the middle of nowhere, first-edition territory for papers in Charleston, Columbia, Savannah and Augusta, which meant what news we got was old and incomplete.

When television did become a part of our lives, it was a fragile, black-and-white version subject to interference from passing planes and thunderstorms.

If there was something important happening out beyond the soybean fields and endless stands of pine trees, it was usually discussed in depth by our fathers as they smoked in the churchyard between Sunday school and church service.

If it was serious, they would grind their cigarette butts harshly into the ground with their shiny shoes before going in to pray. If it was frivolous, they would flip them casually into the bushes, laughing in billows of smoke as they joined our mothers to find their usual place in the pews.

From ground level, theirs appeared to be a simple life where everybody worked hard and hoped their skinny little kids would never have to endure the bloodshed they saw in Europe, Africa and the Pacific.

They had already seen true heroism and therefore didn't need sportswriters to try and cheapen it with stories of ballplayers.

I never heard them refer to a game as war. They knew the difference. That was a word they seldom used, in fact, preferring to look ahead rather than behind. Victory in those days was an air conditioner, a dishwasher, a not-so-used car.

It was having friends and raising children and paying your bills. If there had been such a thing as credit cards, they would not have used them. They saved. They tithed. They gave blood.

To the best of my knowledge, my father only spent one night away from home the whole time I knew him.

He went to Peoria for a seminar and brought my mother back a present which she still has.

I know there were problems that I couldn't see from my vantage point, but what I could see was good and solid and straightforward.

They did not see sports figures of their day as idols, just lucky boys who were paid to continue their adolescence.

They had fought beside better and seen them die young. If they envied Mickey Mantle, it was only for his smile and smooth swing. They thought Yogi Berra was funny. But they did not want to be either one.

To me, these men were my heroes. They were always clean-shaven and smelled of Aqua Velva and Lucky Strikes. They went to work early and came home on time to home-cooked meals.

Many of them are gone now, including my father. Those who aren't must wonder what happened to the world they thought they were creating from the ashes of the war.

A Porch Light Goes Out in a Writer's Life

Three days before Christmas, Dan said goodbye to Judy for the last time. There had been so many goodbyes over the years because coming and going is just the way sportswriters live. But this one was different. It was their last.

For more than 40 years, Dan Foster has been the sports columnist of The Greenville News, a voice that echoes out of the foothills with reason and humor. And for all of those 40 years, he had a partner, a woman who was always there when he came dragging in late at night after ballgames, someone who always left the porch light burning.

Over the years, some of us who bounce from ballyard to ballyard had the pleasure of knowing Judy Foster, Dan's better half. She was one of those rare women who can put up with this vagabond way of life, this extended boyhood that we call work.

It takes someone special to live with a man who travels across country to see a single ballgame, and stays a week. A man who works nights and weekends. A man who's likely to spend more holidays with other reporters than his family. A man who is better at putting his feelings into print than spoken words.

Somehow Judy Foster was the best I've ever known at doing all that. A librarian by trade, she had long ago figured out the difference between ego and false pride, fact and fiction, the importance of the unimportant.

On the road, you can tell the guys who are blessed with good marriages. They are the lucky ones. They have more fun, not the kind you think, but the kind that is real.

If there is a way to endure regular separation, it is through true love, that invisible connection that follows you out of the door, tucks you into strange beds, talks to you on the telephone late at night and welcomes you home with a smile.

Sportswriting, of course, is not the only occupation that requires this kind of magic, but it is one of them. There really is no game on this earth worth saying goodbye for. It is, after all, just a job, and jobs require sacrifice. That's why they're called jobs.

But no matter where we were or what we were doing, I always thought Dan had the best of it. His happiness was secured, his life held together by a woman who kept things going in his absence.

Not just in recent years, when he had achieved his success and earned his place on the page, but through the early years when things were harder. When his sons were young. When they struggled to make ends meet.

There were times, I'm sure, when Judy and the boys would much rather have had him home than have his picture delivered to them on their doorstep.

On a whole, I would say, sportswriters are a lonely bunch, forever surrounded by a crowd. No matter the place or the game, they are always at war with the words.

On one hand they are given the chance to tell the story their way.

On the other they are never sure they can. And during the long in-betweens, they wait for other people to do something so they can try.

If there is a payoff, it comes when a reader chuckles or frowns at a breakfast table far away. And that may be enough, a small deposit in a long-term account that we like to call a career.

In most cases, however, we find ourselves writing for an audience of one. That one person back

home who is dealing with diapers and dishwashers and clogged drains, but takes a moment on the phone to say the story was good, everything is fine, they miss you and can't wait until you get home.

That is what makes a deadline phrase worth turning. That is what keeps a man going.

This past year, when Judy was losing her battle against breast cancer, we missed Dan at a few of the big events. The Final Four and The Masters weren't quite the same without his smiling face in the press room.

We knew, however, that he was with Judy. Holding her hand as each treatment brought promise, only to fail.

At her funeral this week, Dan was strong and handsome in his grief, and friends from every trail he'd wandered came to pay their respects.

A good many were fellow sportswriters, guys who knew better than most what Dan had lost. A friend, a partner, a smile, a laugh, a porch light that was always burning.

When Fathers Cry For Sons Left Behind

There is no sadness as deep or as dark as the one that slips in when I see fathers playing with their sons. Sometimes it is like a black hole that I dare not fall into for fear of being lost forever in that pain.

Those simple games of catch. That moment of explanation on something as complex as a curveball. The look of understanding they share when the concept of the infield-fly rule becomes clear.

Sports, for many fathers and sons, can be the one lifelong connection that allows them a closeness they otherwise might never know.

It bonds the flesh and spirit. It renews the soul. There is something there that overlaps the seasonal beginnings and ends and stretches beyond statistics and details. It is a secret club without mothers and sisters. Time spent outside the realms of school and work. A place that is like no other.

You can see it so clearly in the Mutt-and-Jeff images of fathers and sons walking to and from games. You can hear it in words that pass between them, the laughter, the learning of the ropes as the soft sounds of knowledge are passed down in generational order.

It is the way things should be, but too often aren't.

I often wonder how many fathers take all this for granted, because I know so many who don't.

In a society where only half of our sons grow up with their fathers, the pain is mathematically squared by the number of fathers growing old without their sons.

Regardless of the reasons for separation and the hopes of maintaining a true relationship over the years, it never seems to turn out the way it should.

You're either a father, or you're not. There is no in-between. There has never been a phone call that could replace a hug, or a Christmas present that meant as much as an afternoon at the ball park.

And for all our excuses of time, distance or financial circumstances, we may never exorcise the guilt that comes with a 9-year-old baseball player in a wallet-sized photograph, who is suddenly 14, and finished with a career you never saw.

In all likelihood, it will be 20 or 30 years before a young boy comes to know the hard realities of life, and that could be much too late for most of us.

And even though we've come to appreciate how mature and flexible children of the '90s can be, we know there are times when they ask themselves why and there is no good answer.

In my case, his name is Brent, and I cannot help but fight back the tears when I think of what he must think of me sometimes. I know there is an anger there that he hides much better than I ever could.

For I stole something from him that no one else can replace, and in turn, I robbed myself in the process. It was not his fault, and blame is not something we have discussed.

Instead, we pass our times together talking peripherally of the latest sporting events I've been covering, carefully joking about how much travel I do and when I'll be passing his way again. Every visit ends with "I love you," but it ends just the same.

I don't write this for sympathy, and it's not to make divorced fathers feel sorry for themselves. We all have our stories.

Instead, this is for the real fathers who are still there, doing the daily stuff that makes them heroes in the eyes of their sons, whether they know it or not.

These are the guys who coach the youth baseball teams, listen to the stories of failure, encourage the dreams and do all the little things that make a boy's childhood whole and seemingly uneventful.

Maybe you don't realize it because it's just the way things are and you haven't noticed it lately because the water pump on the car needs fixing and the house needs painting and your wife thinks you need to lose a few pounds in the new year.

Or maybe even you haven't spent as much time with him as you should since you've been worried about things at work, or because he's going through an irritable stage.

Sometimes it's hard. Really hard. And there is no hall of fame for those who pull it off. There are, however, a lot of little rewards that sometimes are easy to overlook.

All the rest of us can say is that if you're taking what you have for granted, please, please, don't.

Looking Back at Allendale 25 Years Later

On the day I finished high school 25 years ago, General William Westmoreland was calling for another 100,000 troops to be sent to Vietnam. A Clint Eastwood spaghetti western was big box office, Doug Clark and the Hot Nuts were playing at the Folly Beach Pier, hometown boy Bob McNair was governor of South Carolina and the Atlanta Braves lost to St. Louis 5-4.

A lot has changed in this rural community since I left, but a lot has remained the same. The field where we played Little League baseball is consumed with weeds, our high school is a middle school and the football field looks tiny and lonesome compared to the brightly lit Friday nights I remember.

There are some stores where there used to be fields and fields where there used to be stores. Time has a way of changing the landscape of your youth.

But for those of us who grew up in these small towns of South Carolina in the '50s and '60s, there is a blood bond, something that makes us all alike in many ways. Something city kids don't understand.

Whether it was Allendale or Barnwell or Hampton or Estill or Williston or Bamberg or Denmark or any of the hundreds of little towns where you might have been raised, there's something that makes you wish you could recreate parts of it and give it to your children for Christmas.

With a shortage of movies and other entertainment, sports was a big part of small-town life. It fit right into a childhood where the main modes of transportation were bicycles and dreams.

Baseball, basketball and football consumed our waking hours, especially during the long summer months, and were never far from our thoughts when we lay down and waited for a sleep-inducing breeze to rustle through the open windows at night.

If there was crime in our early lives we did not know about it. Nobody locked their doors at night or when they went to the beach on vacation. We knew where the jailhouse was but didn't know who was inside.

It was an idyllic, childlike existence protected from the outside world by miles and miles and miles

of farmland. Seventy miles from the nearest city, a million miles for almost everything else.

And in this hot, humid cocoon of a world we were incubated into becoming the kind of Americans our parents wanted us to be.

We did not know what the '60s would do to us when we left the ballfields of our childhood behind. We had no way of knowing. We simply walked into a world that was changing and we changed with it.

We were, however, children of television. Most of us remember when they rolled the beautiful beasts into our homes.

We knew Howdy Doody and Pinky Lee and Dizzy Dean, never realizing there was a difference between what we could see on the fuzzy screen or through the screen on our front door.

Yankee Stadium where Pee Wee Reese and Mickey Mantle and Whitey Ford played was as accessible as the field across the street where we played. One you got to by flicking a switch, the other by slamming the back door behind you and promising to be home by suppertime.

Neither seemed important at the time, for time was something we had in abundance and filled the way all little boys do, any way we could. There was, you see, no point of reference to what was important and what was not. The World Series, in our minds, weighed in as heavily as a six-man game of softball down the street.

As we grew older, a Friday night of high school football followed by a dance at the armory had more meaning than a Super Bowl because all those people lived in a box in our living rooms.

They did not live in Ulmer or Sycamore or Kline or go to church with us or have kids in our class, so they really didn't exist as far as we were concerned.

Now, 25 years later, I'm back here for my high school reunion and I know much more about what is real and what isn't.

I've been to Super Bowls, Final Fours, World Series, Masters and all the other things that television brings to kids today in a box, and I know the difference.

The real stuff, despite the weeds and neglect, is the ballfield where I learned to steal second; the lonely football field where I learned the true meaning of sweat; and all the little unmarked fields where my childhood friends and I invented games with rules that changed by the day.

All of us are products of our childhood, no matter where and how we grew up. It gives us perspective, allows us to see with different eyes.

And now, with the hindsight of time, there is nothing about mine that I would change.

GOLF

Golf in the Lowcountry Is Something Special

There is an ageless mist that gathers and hangs on the marsh at dawn until the summer sun burns it away and leaves behind a steamy day that only a golfer can love.

Along the same soggy edges of America where life began in its primal form and rice and indigo once paid for lifestyles that now linger only in old houses and memories, the sacred silence of morning accepts the flight of a well-struck ball as gently as the flush of osprey wings.

To know that feeling, to be able to close your eyes on rainy days and dark nights and re-create it in your mind, is to know golf in the Lowcountry.

For a course laid gently down between the past and present is a golfer's reason to believe in the future.

It is not as essential as love or as trivial as loneliness, but it fills a void left somewhere along the way when we traded serenity for progress.

Although it is a game because it has rules, it is also art because it's painted on the everchanging canvas of nature's breast.

All sport is spent in search of special moments that make the effort worthwhile. They are spaced sparingly between preparation and desperation, but they are there.

The geometric beauty of a spinning spiral that finds its way into soft, waiting hands. The clothy clap that punctuates a perfect jump shot. The human acceptance when a fastball illuminates the invisibility of the outside corner.

In golf, it comes quietly during those few seconds of flight. That suspended moment between effort and realization when Earth has no hold nor jurisdiction and hope rides a small white rocket into space.

We have no drug that can produce that singular sensation.

In modern life, there is the magic of birth, the longing of true love, the wisdom of age and the purity of a perfectly struck 6-iron.

Everything else is manufactured.

In the timescope of man, the long and storied history of golf is only a half-tick on the clock without

numbers. When all is written, it may not merit a footnote.

But in the here and now, along the South Carolina coast, it has consumed several generations of effort, transformed pastures into putting greens and created a cash crop whose value is generally unaffected by global market trends or wars or the endless movements of soldiers across the globe.

For on any given day, there may be more than 50,000 golfers spread out over the 2500 holes that stretch and curve along our coastline—old soldiers who have walked away from war and young men who think they know what it's like, but don't.

On these plush fairways, however, their battles are harmless endeavors where they inflict pain only on themselves. They hit, but no one is injured. They shoot, but no one falls. Among the many games man has concocted through time for his amusement few are as individually dramatic or devastating.

For it is a game played against the mirror of one's ability. It leaves no bloody victims behind.

When the battle is over, the battlefield bears no bodies. All the soldiers survive.

And with nightfall comes a natural armistice, a cease-fire of sorts when darkness plays through in a foursome with the earth's natural tilt, spin and rotation.

A time for soldiers to reload, regroup and replenish their hopes.

For in the millenium of time, the next one will be the best one and the soldiers will return, ready to attack. In fierce battles that will never make the history books of time.

Although there are golf balls resting this very day on the surface of the moon, this fact does not verify the game's universal appeal.

Nor does the fact that there are many more resting on the sandy bottoms of many small lagoons mean that the game belongs here on the earth. It is, however, an evolutionary social product of our times, and these fossilized spheres should bring smiles to future faces we will never know a thousand years from now.

But if a single thing should somehow survive the fire and ice of time and we are considered curiously by our descendants as a people that engaged in a game of hit and hunt, we can only hope they realize where the endeavor occurred and why.

For on some days of our lives we need to put ourselves among the moss-laden oaks that wall the soft-graced lakes and guide us through a place and time that won't last forever.

Sooner or later the morning mists will cover our tracks in the marshlands, and when the summer sun burns it clean we will be gone.

But until then, we have something special here in the Lowcountry. And it is called golf.

You Can Tell a Lot About a Man by His Golf Game

He didn't wear the latest pro shop clothes or have the best set of clubs. He didn't talk the country club line or come to the course with a string of off-color jokes.

He didn't move his ball in the rough or conveniently forget to count a stroke when he duffed one in the sand trap. He faced the golf course like a legitimate challenge and did not try to cheat fate.

He didn't take advantage of his expense account or his corporate position. He didn't take cheap shots at his superiors behind their backs or deride his competition unfairly.

He wasn't loud or obnoxious or overbearing. He moved across the course with a confident stride regardless of the previous shot. He was the same man after nailing a drive down the middle as when a testy wedge shot strayed wide of the green.

If he had a temper, it was as controlled as his putting stroke. He saw humor in the shortcomings of his short game and truly appreciated the beauty of a fairway wood well hit. He was competitive, but winning was not the reason he played.

His etiquette around the ball was seasoned with a natural maturity, pristine in its absence of spoiled-boy horseplay and unnecessary needling. He knew and respected the rules. He understood the written and unwritten rules of the game and showed a genuine respect for those around him.

He played with a calm that comes with inner confidence. He knew the course was designed to test his skill and not to destroy his will. He admired the subtle impossibilities built into the land and never felt he was cheated by the creators. He took advantage of the course where it allowed, but accepted its inevitable direction and flow.

He kept pleasure and disappointment on an even scale. The sweet click of a well-connected three iron was reflected directly in his eyes. A misread putt that hung stubbornly on the lip became a study in perfection rather than a reason to riot.

From green to tee he was a man at peace with himself. He knew the wind and water were part of the test. He did not play his opponents, but put himself up against the course as it lay.

Between shots he spoke of good times and bad, but never sold himself as something he was not. His family and work were foremost in his life. His golf shots were crisp and disciplined. He went for the pin, knowing they may not fall, but always giving himself a chance to succeed. He was not a dreamer, but a realist on and off the course.

He did not change when conversations swept lightly between golf and business. He could read greens and financial reports with equal aptitude, applying the proper significance to each.

He did not balk at a friendly wager, but enjoyed the extra edge it gave to the game. He would have paid up generously had he lost, but his game made him a humble recipient. He did not gloat or grind his victims down. He praised their effort without a condescending tone.

He spoke to clubhouse boys and bartenders with the same respect he offered his corporate counterparts. His demeanor attracted special attention, but he did not expect it.

There are a lot of eyebrows raised when men take to the links for a day and call it business. But there are many intangible things that can be learned about a person during a four-hour round of golf.

I could tell by the time we finished, he was an honest man.

Golfing in a Cathedral at Twilight

As the parking lot thins out and the day's light begins to wane, the sound of a tee shot splits the silence and a lone player begins what is known to most as golf at its best.

With twilight hanging on the horizon, imminent in its destination toward darkness, he walks the fairway in a singular motion, oblivious to the death of day and whatever problems die slowly with it.

To be the only player on a golf course late in the afternoon during these autumnal days blessed with an extra hour of light is to walk in a private cathedral of sight and sound.

It is a time when long shadows lean across greens like ghostly arms, sand traps deepen beneath the shade of their own treachery and each breath of breeze brings with it the chill of evening arriving earlier and earlier.

But to the golfer, there is always time for an emergency nine. That therapeutic walk with one's inner self. A choreographed stroll through the soul that puts the game of golf and life in proper perspective.

Void of the chatter and chicanery that often accompany the game when electric carts roll in convoys down the fairways, golf in the twilight is almost a religious experience.

As dusk degrades itself in shades of gray, the flight of a white ball through the changing air onto the dark green expanse of an inviting fairway is something artists struggle to capture.

And there are the sounds, or lack of them, that make you strain to hear things so often drowned out by the rattling of clubs and beer cans and jokes you've heard a thousand times before.

So seldom do you hear the sound of your own footsteps, the subtle scrunch a tee makes when entering the ground, the flop of a far-flung divot or the purring sound a putt makes as it breaks against the grain.

It is a time when you can actually hear yourself breathe before you take the club back, and exhale as you follow its flight.

And off in the distance, if you concentrate and focus, you can hear the ball land as softly as an egret near the target of your dreams.

Perhaps the best part of the twilight round is not the game itself, but the stretches of solitude that come between shots.

Walking quietly through the tee-to-green numerical maze in fading light is similar to finding your way around your house in the middle of the night. You don't have to see what you know is there.

You feel the presence of obstacles. You know how many steps there are between things.

You are never lost. The smell of honeysuckle acknowledges the edge of safety to the left. The pungency of pluff mud exposed by a receding tide warns of danger to the right.

Even sand has a scent. So does water.

As does the dew, which you can almost hear forming on the grass as the last points of light give way to the oncoming night.

As the last tee shot is struck on the home hole, it disappears into a darkness illuminated only by the glimmer of light from the distant clubhouse where the hangers-on are playing liars' poker and drinking beer.

The only other point of reference is the spraying and swerving sounds the cartboys make as they wash, park and recharge the carts for the next day's rounds.

By now, visual line of flight gives way to mental radar. With all other senses on full alert, the ball is tracked by the feel of a push or pull.

Even without seeing it, your mind's eye squints to follow what you cannot.

And somehow, without your knowing how, the ball appears dimly in the fairway where you thought it might be.

And with the last flag flapping vaguely against the stained-glass hues of a sunset gone, the twilight golfer relies on instinct instead of sprinkler heads, fires with faith and listens for the soft sound of a green hit in regulation.

That, followed by the plunk of the ball as it falls into the final cup, is where the twilight journey ends in total darkness.

A perfect round of solitude and silence, hailed only by the applause of crickets.

OF GRASS AND KIDS

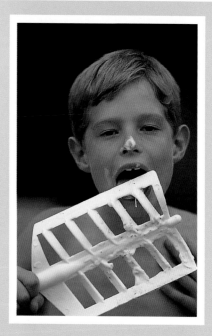

Of Grass and Kids and What It All Means

There is a path that runs alongside our house where small boys and dogs routinely scamper by en route to adventures that lie somewhere in the mysterious netherworld beyond our backyard.

On almost any given day, and especially on weekends, the shrubbery is rustled and tiny footsteps can be heard romping past as a clandestine herd of tow-headed village children cut the corners of parental boundaries and make their own way through the neighborhood.

Occasionally, they will pause long enough in the backyard to throw a ball or wrestle with each other in the new-mown grass. Then they disappear as quickly as they came through a hole in the fence that leads to someone else's yard. Their sudden presence has often frightened my wife, who has to spend too much time at home alone.

And their constant passage is no bargain for the grass we work so hard to nurture in the name of keeping up with the Joneses.

There was even a fleeting thought of sealing off the passageway, a move that would force the kids to take the long way around to wherever they were going.

But as I pondered such a drastic measure, I remembered something my own father said years ago, and took no action.

Not a particularly sensitive man, my father did possess a keen sense of what it was like to be a kid.

When we were young, our backyard was a large expanse of treeless grass that was often transformed into football and baseball fields depending on the season. It attracted many of the neighborhood kids, especially when he installed a basketball goal in the far corner for us to use. The yard, of course, took a terrible pounding, and there was a time when my mother expressed concern and thought perhaps our friends could be persuaded to take their games elsewhere.

"They are ruining the grass," she said, not to mention the flower beds and shrubbery she tried to keep in presentable condition.

But in his ultimate wisdom, my father simply said no, explaining in a gentle way what it was like to be a little boy at play in a world confined to what was available.

"The grass will come back in time," he told my mother. "But the children will be gone."

Sure enough, we grew up and the grass grew back as if we had never been there at all. There remains, however, that magical memory of the neighborhood where we roamed at will through everybody's yard, using secret passageways and hideouts that were designed for other purposes.

But there were always one or two yards that were off limits. People who cherished their horticultural habitats more than the wide-eyed wonderment of children galloping on make-believe horses into unseen battles.

These were the people we loved to torment at a distance, occasionally trespassing on their precious lawns for the simple sake of raising their ire and hearing them yell at us as we rode away on imaginary steeds to destinations that existed only in our fertile and devilish minds.

These are the people we swore we would never grow up to be.

For every young boy, regardless of where he grew up, knows that the sacred and open range of a neighborhood should always be free to roam at will.

In today's world, I suppose I should be concerned about insurance and liability and other things that could come from the free flow of other people's children through our property.

But the little boy in me only sees young warriors traipsing down old Indian trails with cowboys in hot pursuit, or army buddies slipping through the underbrush, giggling about their ability to hide from those who seek.

And if, in the process, our grass doesn't grow exactly the way it should or the shrubbery is bent or broken, I cannot find it in my heart to close off a highway to adventure that some have grown too old to understand.

The grass, after all, will come back in its own good time. But the children, someday, will not.

He's the Best Little Brother I Never Had

As the youngest of two boys in my family, I never had a little brother. Mine, in fact, was a childhood blessed with one of the best big brothers around.

Although Frank was seven years older, he did more things right for me than I'm sure he realizes. Today he is 50 years old and lives far away, but the kindness and caring of decades is always there.

About as close as I can come to sharing that kind of kinship has been with a young Mount Pleasant boy named Latifi (pronounced Lateef), even though we are from different worlds and generations.

When I met Latifi almost three years ago, I thought I was somehow giving something back to the community. It was a gallant gesture, I thought, the right thing to do.

I soon learned, however, that life has a funny way of turning things around. And now, as we've both grown older, I think he has taught me more than I've taught him.

Latifi was 13 when we were matched through the Big Brother/Big Sister program sponsored by the Carolina Youth Development Center.

Born and raised in New York City, his only memory of his father was a photograph of a handsome man in a military uniform who had passed away before he was born.

Since then, life had dealt him another bad hand. His mother was dying of an incurable disease. I met her in her waning days as she had moved back to South Carolina to die and leave her only son in the care of her aging mother, Ida.

During those somber days, I would pick Latifi up for movies or a ballgame, never knowing quite what to say or what to do for him. Mostly we talked of everything except the obvious. His hopes and dreams. Baseball. Football. How he was doing in school.

When his mother died, I was out of town. When I returned, he had handled things better than most grownups I have known. I was proud of him, but still didn't know him any better than I knew myself.

Over the years, I have made the same mistakes most real big brothers make. I haven't always been there when I should have been. Work and travel have always been handy excuses.

And, in striving to focus his attention toward improving his grades, I took the easy way out—I bribed him—and it worked. A computer game for Bs. A Charlotte Hornets jacket for As.

I'm convinced now that the bribes were probably unnecessary. Latifi is a bright and pleasant fellow dealt a hand most people would fold quickly and blame the dealer.

To his credit, he has not. He has involved himself in sports and life and smiles as if he is the luckiest boy in the world.

I sometimes wish I could take some credit for Latifi, but that would be selfish. His true strength comes from the handsome man in an old photograph and a mother who left him in the loving hands of a grandmother who cares.

I am fortunate in the fact that Latifi has always been a better Little Brother than I am a Big Brother. He doesn't employ guilt as a weapon. He takes things in stride.

Throughout our community, however, there are hundreds of men and women volunteering their time in the Big Brother/Big Sister program who do it better than I, and each has a story to tell.

For the most part, they are the unsung heroes among us whose commitment is real and whose rewards are personal. They are folks from every walk of life who believe a few hours a week might help change a life. And they are willing to try.

Last night I handed Latifi a baseball as he threw out the first pitch at a Rainbows game. His smile made me feel as if I had given him the world on a platter, when actually the opposite is true.

Someday, I hope to stand back in the shadows as he moves on through college and into a wonderful life. And if somehow a picnic or a computer game or a night at College Park made a difference, it will be because he was the best little brother I never had.

# A Tip of the Baseball Cap to Single Moms

She is the one sitting in the stands with the oversized pocketbook, a look of loneliness hidden behind her smile and a sense of insecurity about when to cheer and when not to.

A single mother of a 10-year-old second baseman, she has worked all day and made it to the game just in time. Her son is at bat. His father is not around.

She does not know that the small boy in the batter's box is too wide in his stance and too high on the handle. She only knows that this is where she must be.

Since the divorce, she has assumed the absent father's role as best she can. She has bought uniforms and shoes. She has tossed batting practice in the backyard. She has bought and sorted baseball cards. She has nursed skinned knees and tried to heal a broken heart.

What she does not know about baseball could fill a book. All she knows for certain is that her son is at bat and she is there, a fact that overrides her innocent lack of knowledge of the game.

At the plate, the little boy sees her out of the corner of his eye. She is always there. Sometimes late, but always there.

That some of his teammates' fathers are coaching his team and passing down the unwritten rules of baseball is a reality not lost on him.

He has a picture of his own dad playing ball when he was a kid, which he keeps hidden in a drawer in his bedroom.

Although his mother knew nothing of how to form a pocket in his new baseball glove, his best friend's father showed him how. And when a ground ball took a bad hop and popped him in the nose, he avoided her motherly concern, preferring to shake it off stoically the way he had seen real ballplayers do it on television.

After school, when there was nobody to play with, he would bounce his ball off the garage wall pretending to make double plays as he waited for her to come home from work. Sometimes it was dark before her car pulled into the driveway.

And there were nights when she let him sleep in his uniform, pretending not to hear him cry when she closed the door to leave him to his dreams.

So as he digs in at the plate, the little boy dares not chance a look to the point high in the stands

where she is sitting. But he knows, without looking, exactly where she is.

In recent years, there have been men in her life who feigned interest in her son's baseball career, tossed him a few balls and patted him on the head as they left.

But the true weight of child-rearing has been hers to bear.

Her ex had been quite an athlete in his time. And it is at times like this that she wishes she had paid more attention during times gone by.

From her vantage point, he looks so small in his baggy uniform, his face barely visible deep within the batting helmet. And from this distance, there is nothing she can do to help him put bat to ball.

But as she clutches her pocketbook, the distinctive ring of his metal bat sends the ball squirting through the infield and like a flash he is down to first base, standing on the bag, safe for the moment.

Her shriek of delight is almost loud enough to embarrass him, but not quite. And as she finds herself standing and applauding, she gets a nod of approval from an older man seated nearby.

A mother's instinct, however, is enough to know the basics. That an umpire's call of strike three deserves a howl. That a coach should not make a little boy cry. That an error is not the end of the world.

And yet there are moments when she yearns for some primal understanding of when and how to console a bruised ego the way men do. A slap on the rump from Mom does not come naturally or carry the same message as one delivered from those who have been there before.

As he swings and misses, she squirms a bit and yells his name with encouragement. Then, he swings and misses again.

As she gathers herself, she stares with pride at the boy on base and wonders what life would have been like if.

Then, in a move so fast that no one could see it but her, the little boy tips the bill of his baseball cap in her direction, and she knows it is as good as it gets.

Rhythm and Blue Jeans Dance on a Rain-splattered Court

Raindrops speckled the asphalt court as he dribbled between the puddles and lofted the ball through a rusted rim that had no net. In blue jeans and sneakers, he had the grace of a dancer performing to a sell-out crowd. But he was quite alone, with raindrops providing the only applause.

I watched him for several minutes from my car, wondering what his life was like. He was in his early teens, black, slender, but not particularly tall. He moved to and from the backboard like a lamb finding its mother in the dark. The ball was almost an unnoticed prop, sliding from hand to hand and seldom touching the ground except for the rhythmic dribble that paced the dance.

Jump shot, set shot, layup, dunk. His choreography had transitional smoothness that comes only with years of rehearsal or natural talent. Between sets, he would drop back from the circle and survey the court with eyes that perceived each filling puddle as a defensive threat. The constant dribble never stopped. It was as sure as his heartbeat.

Then, with sweet subtlety, he faked left and right and rose into the air like an eagle leaving its perch. At the peak of the leap, where gravity combats desire, his hands flipped the ball effortlessly toward the basket. Anywhere else, the ball's flight would have followed its fall through the rim. But here it splattered unceremoniously to the ground.

By this time, I was in awe. He continued to shoot and spin and elude whoever his imagination decided was in the way. His shots were crisp and true and seldom off the mark. His biggest enemy was the old rim that wobbled on its base and looked as if it were one rusted bolt from falling off.

Taking a chance and following an urge, I opened the car door and strolled slowly to the fence that separated us. His eyes picked me up like a fast break forming off a rebound. He kept shooting, and hitting, but never lost sight of my moves.

I leaned against a post near the gate entrance and assumed a non-threatening pose. He eyed me warily as he lofted layups from side to side. I shifted

my weight from left to right and he broke away from the basket like a shot, guarding the ball with a staccato dribble that sounded like a marching band was coming around the corner. I folded my arms and kept my distance.

By now the rain was falling harder. Neither of us seemed to care. He was in his favorite place and I was honored to be there. Our only eye contact came in quick acknowledgments of purity after his shots jangled through the rim over and over again. He never spoke, and neither did I.

I knew by instinct this was not my place. It was his. This potholed parking lot of a basketball court was where he reigned. I was an outsider who fell from the sky, a faceless stranger like all the others who whiz by in cars on the nearby interstate.

As I drifted off in these thoughts, I almost didn't see it coming. In fact, I must have heard it first—the sound of a missile cutting through heavy air. Before I knew it , I whirled and caught the ball he zipped my way. In the distance I saw him smile for a moment, then drop down in a defensive stance before the basket.

The ball felt strange in my hands. It was old and smooth and all the lettering had long since worn away. But it was tight, like a powerful machine that should not be driven by amateurs.

I bounced it once to get the feel. Again to get confidence. Then slowly I worked my way across the back edge of the court as he followed my every move. This was obviously no contest, but the adrenaline was pumping.

I made an easy move to the left and his body turned toward me like a tank turret. I moved right and felt the heat of his radar. I looked to the basket and

70

his body was everywhere I wanted to go. In desperation I threw up a jump shot.

It was off by several feet. He snagged it in the air, smiled quickly, and bounced it back to me. I drove right for a layup, but his young hands flashed like lightning and stole the ball before I left the ground. He smiled. I shot. He smiled again.

In another place, another time, my embarrassment would have shown. But on his court there was no place for it. I settled for shagging his rebounds and watching him perform up close.

As darkness closed in, he circled the court one last time, drove lazily towards the basket and stuffed it in backwards. Before I could applaud, he spun the ball triumphantly on his index finger and dribbled away—the sound of his heartbeat echoing in the night.

She Didn't Know Sports, But She Knew Little Boys

She was always there when I needed her. I don't think she knew a strike from a ball or a touchdown from a touchback, but she knew how to heal a little boy's heart when it was broken.

And it was she who left her supper on the stove to come out into the back yard and throw grounders when Dad was working late. And she never complained about the never-ending pile of dirty uniforms that kept her busy in the laundry room.

She knew how important a pair of spiked baseball shoes were, and pitched in a few bucks for their purchase when my allowance came up short. And when a tired team of dirty-faced boys showed up on the back porch, she always found cookies and Koolaid, no matter how close it was to suppertime.

When my muscles were so sore I could hardly sleep, she soothed the pain with magic lotion and the loving touch of her hands. She would usually find a way to attend the games when Dad was too busy, and she never tired of busing a noisy group of boys back and forth from practice.

Somehow she understood when I used her big barrel of laundry detergent to line off our neighborhood baseball field, and she didn't tell Dad about the time I cried when I struck out four times.

She knew I could not cry in front of my father when I failed in sports, and she had a way of making me feel like a winner when nobody else could.

For mothers have an innate notion about little boys and the games they play. They do not need to know the rules of the game to share the glory or the pain. They instinctively find a way to make the good times better, the bad times pass. When it came time to play the rougher game of football, she could see in my soul that it was a necessary test of manhood, and never told anyone of the sobs she heard coming from my room at night.

I know she worried and prayed that I would not get hurt, but she never embarrassed me in front of my friends. She would deliberately look away when the hard hits were thrown, finding a way to smile when I walked away in one piece.

There were times when I think the bumps and bruises hurt her more than me. Once or twice I thought I saw her about to cry out in anger, but she never did. Mothers can feel things others can't feel.

As the boys got bigger and the games got tougher, she never tried to hold me back. There were always stories of my father's childhood injuries and exploits in sports and she knew I could expect noth-

73

ing less of myself. Mothers know what sons must do to survive.

But when things were good, I didn't share it with her. I regret that.

It was Dad I talked to about the home runs or the diving catches. I would run to him for approval and congratulations. He would pat me on the back and tell me I was doing well. A chip off the old block. A boy passing into manhood.

But when times were bad, it was always Mom who came through. Dad and I would talk about it, but I could feel his disappointment and the conversations were short. When I walked away, it was Mom who would mend the wounds and make me feel good about myself.

She knew how to change the subject or find something good to say about my performance. She had a way of making a warm bath and a pot roast worthy reward for a boy's efforts on the field.

I never realized how much she meant to a little boy struggling to be what others expected him to be. She had a hug that made me feel like a champion and a smile that allowed me to try again.

There weren't many trophies, but if I still had one, I'd give it to her today.

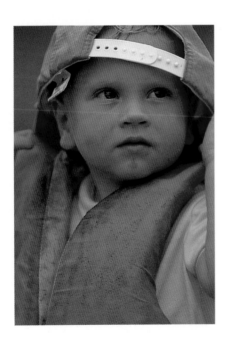

AGAINST THE ODDS

Sea Island Girl Beats the Odds

Quantia Singleton is a child of the Sea Islands, equally kissed and cursed by the soft marshlands of Yonge's Island and the hard times that are part of the rural, black South.

In many ways, she is no different from her friends. At the tender age of 18, Quantia has a 1-year-old son, Diondra, whose father keeps a safe distance. And she has seen her share of violence, a fact of life she wears like a badge in the form of a scar from a nasty razor cut on her left arm that took 300 stitches to close.

She was lucky that day, however, in that the girl who slashed at her with a box cutter missed her neck, which was her intended target.

Still, despite childbirth and serious injury, Quantia is set to graduate from Baptist Hill High School soon, and eventually, she hopes to graduate from college. She has decent grades and says they're getting better.

But Quantia has one thing going for her that most of her friends do not. Quantia, you see, can throw a shotput and sling a discus like no other. And that, she realizes, is what makes her special.

Her coach at the small class AA school south of Charleston is John Locke, who after four years of coaching Quantia says she is a natural and could be one of the best.

Since the eighth grade, the 5'8" 180-pound girl has been named the most valuable athlete in the county track meet every year. For three straight years she has placed first in discus and shotput in the Lower State meets and at least first or second in the state finals. And she is an all-star basketball player, leading her team in rebounds.

"When she got pregnant, I thought she was finished," Locke said of his prize athlete, "but she came back within six weeks of having her baby. Then, when she got cut so badly, I thought she was finished, but she came back from that, too. Quantia bounces back from everything. She just keeps coming back. She never gives up."

Locke says she displays that same kind of mental toughness in competition. "If you beat Quantia by an inch, she'll come back and beat you by an inch," he said. "She can raise it up another notch when she has to."

Like a lot of kids who grow up in small, country communities, however, being a track and field star was not high on her list of ambitions when she was in middle school.

She went out for the teams to kill some of the time that builds up in the marshland like moss on the trees. Locke, in fact, said distances and lack of transportation are two of his students' biggest hardships.

"We've got some phenomenal athletes sitting under trees after school because they don't have rides to practices," he said.

That and the lack of proper weight-room equipment and other things are just part of the reason an athlete like Quantia Singleton is unique. Still, her reasons for wanting to compete on a higher level are just starting to come into focus.

"At first I went out for sports because I didn't want to sit at home," She said. "Then I saw that if you're good at something, people look up to you. Now, people from all over the state know who I am, and that's nice."

College recruiters, in fact, have been in contact with Quantia, hoping to bring her 38-foot, 7-inch shotput throw and 135-5 discus hurl to their campuses where they can take her raw talent and improve it even further.

Until recently college wasn't a top priority for Quantia Singleton. Growing up hard and fast, however, changed that.

"I've learned that life is about how far you want to go," Quantia said. "Before Diondra was born, sports was the only thing on my mind. Now, I have responsibilities at home and have to make choices. And nine out of 10 times, the baby wins.

"It's a busy life, but I've got support from my family. Life's not easy out here without support. But now I see that I've got a chance. But without Diondra, college wouldn't be on my mind. Now, I think of what it will be like when he's going to Baptist Hill High and he sees my name on the wall for all the things I did. It sort of changes your attitude about things."

To the point where Quantia Singleton, a child of the Sea Islands, can now see beyond the marshy bluffs that have been her life on Yonge's Island. She has learned there is a life out there beyond how far she can throw a discus, and perhaps because of how far she can throw a discus.

They Run and Ride Until They Catch Themselves

The morning is perfumed with a mixture of sweet sweat and grassy dew, both evaporating quickly as the runners make the first turn of the biathlon, a self-imposed, self-fulfilling torture test of the '90s.

Run five kilometers, bike 20 miles, run another five kilometers.

As the Sunday morning sun burns down on the 300 entered at Stono Ferry, they grunt and groan and pant as they pad down the quiet streets, urging each other on, wanting only to find the strength to beat the one just ahead of them.

Because the spectrum of age and talent within the Charleston Triathlon Club is diverse. Young and old. Male and female. Gifted and gutsy. They come from all walks of life, brought together by this mild madness, those who have endured the passing fancy of running and made it a part of their lives.

Yuppies, mostly. Nice cars. Nice jobs. Nice families. No harm in that.

They are the people whose wrist watches beep for important business meetings during the week, and track pulse rates and quarter-mile times on the weekends.

They are the quiet athletes of America, filling the gap between the money madness on the tube and child-worship on the playgrounds.

For the most part, they are the former body abusers of the '60s and '70s, converted and determined to reverse the damage done in their youth.

They are enlightened.

Somewhere between puberty and parenting they rejected the idea that they would live a life of excess and regret only to die without knowing why. So they looked deep into the black hole of alternatives and found another way.

They started eating better and taking better care of themselves. And they started running out of sheer terror. And they ran until the tears streamed into their ears and it hurt so much that it felt good.

And it was then, and only then, when the pain clouded the brain, that running made sense. They realized that running is a legal drug. Not easily obtained. Not cheap. Not destructive.

A drug for the '90s and beyond. Acceptable. Almost elitist. Environmentally safe. So this is what they do. And why they do it.

The field of runners on this day at Stono Ferry is like a meadow of mixed flowers, each blooming in its own spectrum of colors, each in its own time.

There are teenagers whose lean bodies don't know what it's like to feel the rust of ruin. They are

the children of the converted who know this only as fun, although their day of rebellion is yet to come.

And there are grandmothers who used to play tennis and softball as little girls until motherhood and male domination forced them to put their athletic ambitions aside. They are the resurrected who have come back to reclaim what they lost.

And there are the middle-aged men who had forgotten or misfiled the joy of competing for competition's sake. They are the ones who run the hardest, trying to outrun a sudden sense of mortality, catch up with their lost youth, prove something to themselves nobody else could understand.

There are as many reasons as there are flowers in the field.

It is, however, a pleasant punishment for those who find it fitting. Events like these are peopled with smiling, supportive faces who know what the others are sacrificing to participate. And there appears to be no real envy of those who can do it better or faster.

Although they clog the starting line to get a jump on the field, they quickly spread out according

to ability. They really aren't racing against each other anyway, only against themselves. And it doesn't matter how long it takes, sooner or later they catch themselves and find out something they didn't know before.

Win or lose, the feelings of satisfaction are the same. We all have a need to do something we don't think we can.

All Graduates Need to Know Life Ain't Easy

I was asked recently to be commencement speaker at the University of South Carolina campus in my hometown of Allendale, which came as a big surprise to me, as I'm sure it does to you.

Sportswriters do not usually don cap and gown and try to tell other people about life. But they asked, so I did.

Not knowing, of course, anything about life other than the one I have lived so far, I chose that as my topic. I also told them that the speech wouldn't last too long because I was going to tell them the truth, which didn't take as long as lying.

After being introduced with information I had supplied, I told the graduates that one of the great things about getting older is that it gives you some latitude in writing your own resume.

Mine, for instance, made me sound like quite a fellow—a college graduate, a hometown boy made good, a successful newspaper columnist.

Then I lifted a list from my coat pocket and told them about the things that had been conveniently left out.

My current resume doesn't mention that I was kicked off the high school newspaper because the principal and I had a disagreement in principle.

Or that I was also kicked off the paper in college. Or that I flunked out of college in my senior year and had to return a year later after military duty and finish my degree.

It also doesn't say anything about the times I got fed up with the newspaper business and felt underappreciated and left to make more money.

It doesn't say that I was a very unsuccessful salesman for six months and went crawling back to the paper for a job.

Or that I left the business again to be public relations director for a savings and loan (of all things) and was fired 18 months later.

Or that I then started my own PR company and went broke a year later.

It also leaves out the part about filing for bankruptcy and the ugliness of three failed marriages and the pain inflicted on three beautiful children along the way.

And then there was the battle with alcohol and how I live each day knowing I'm just a Jack Daniels on the rocks away from a slow and undignified death.

Over the years, you learn to write around stuff like that when you start rehashing your life, but it's always there if you know how to read between the lines.

I told these young graduates all this stuff about myself because I thought they needed to hear that all success stories are not fairy tales.

Very few people I know have followed a predetermined path to where they are today. There are bends and crossroads and forks in the road that seem to come along with great regularity in life.

Some decisions you get to make and some are made for you, while some things just happen no matter what you do.

I, for instance, had always assumed that successful people did all the right things at the right times and were either the smartest or the luckiest people in the world.

But it doesn't always work that way.

Sometimes the best-laid plans get shelved. Sometimes options narrow. Sometimes opportunities arise in the strangest places.

If we all knew then what we know now, we might change our college majors to flexibility, for that's what it takes to survive in the world today.

Technology is moving so fast that a job you think you want might not even exist five years from now. And if you are young and going into a profession because somebody said you could make a lot of money, you are doing if for all the wrong reasons.

The trick to life, I tell my children today, is to figure out what you like to do and then get somebody to pay you to do it. If that sounds too simple, then maybe it just is.

In my wildest dreams I never thought I would be a sportswriter. I didn't even consider it an option. But the love of my life is writing and somehow, over time, this has evolved.

Will I be doing it for the rest of my life? I don't know.

If nothing else, I've learned that nothing is forever.

We'll all Remember Where We Were When It Started

It began as a whisper. A large crowd was gathering in McAlister Field House to watch The Citadel take on Duke in a basketball game that was as predetermined as the day's news.

"It's started," the word spread. "It's started."

Nobody had to ask what had started. For months, weeks, days and hours the world had been preparing itself for those two words that meant the war in the Middle East had begun. And now it had.

Thirty minutes before the tipoff of a game between a David and Goliath of college basketball, everybody took a firm grip on his emotions and hoped the war would be as predictable.

Just before the game began, the crowd had swollen to 6,000, the largest ever to gather in Charleston for a basketball game. At that moment, The Citadel's public address announcer told the assembled crowd that the president had just announced that the liberation of Kuwait had begun.

There was a sustained and standing ovation by the crowd. Especially the young cadets who cheered the news as if it were the final score.

They are too young to know it has just begun.

I suppose we all will someday remember where we were when we heard that U.S. and Allied Air Forces were entering Iraqi airspace and an operation named "Desert Shield" became a war named "Desert Storm."

At the moment I heard it, I was torn by the fact that I was at a basketball game. An insignificant basketball game.

All my news instincts told me to get up and leave and find something useful to write about. The world is turning over and I was relegated to watching a game which I knew would be lost in the wake of world events.

Then I turned and looked through the crowd behind me. Other people were struggling with the same emotion. You could see it in their faces. Feel it stirring through the crowd. Then I saw a friend who I knew had a son in the Persian Gulf. He was sitting tight. He didn't move.

I walked over and spoke to him and he said he was concerned, but knew there was nothing he could do but pray.

Then a lady appeared at my shoulder. We had met before. I noticed she was wearing the pin of the

82nd Airborne on her blouse. She said her son, too, was in the gulf. In harm's way. We spoke for a few moments and she returned to her seat.

At first I couldn't understand the calm I had seen in their eyes. The players were warming up as they always do before a game. The cheerleaders were cheering as they always do. But something was different.

A few moments later, Peggy Sineath walked to center court and began singing the national anthem.

I have been to a thousand games, all of which rendered that song a thousand different ways. But on this night I heard it clearly for the first time in a long, long time.

The crowd, now fully informed of the moment, joined boldly in the singing. A large American flag hung from the rafters of the field house and the building was suddenly filled with a feeling that brought it all together at once.

I listened to the words. I saw people singing our awkward anthem as if they could somehow guide our pilots home safely or protect our troops with its words.

It was all they had. And at that moment, it was all they needed.

Then there was a moment of silent prayer for those who were suddenly thrust into battle. And it was a very silent moment. Deafening. The kind of silence that screams out loud. The kind that makes you listen to your breath to make sure you're still part of where you are.

It was different, I felt, because of where I was and what I saw.

Directly across from me was the bulk of the corps of cadets. The young boys we see every day around town in their gray uniforms and tight haircuts. I looked at them closely during that quiet moment. They looked even younger than I imagined. And yet, half a world away, boys who were cadets a few years earlier were undoubtedly strapped into sleek bombers, slicing through the Arabian night on a mission of World Order.

Somewhere on campus there were plaques bearing the names of other cadets who had fought and died in previous wars. They probably walk past them every day. I don't think anybody ever stops to read the names. They might today.

Before I could walk away into an uncertain night, the game began as scheduled. There was no discussion of calling it

off. Real life things go as planned. Wars don't.

As expected, the nationally ranked Blue Devils of Duke demolished The Citadel, 83-50. It was close for a while. The underdog Bulldogs put up a gallant fight, even led by five points early on. But eventually, gradually the much taller and talented prevailed.

There was a sense of relief when it was over. What had been a much-publicized appearance of a team like Duke coming to The Citadel will now and forever only be remembered as the night the war

began. Everybody hurried home to find out the details.

As I walked out into the night air, anxious to catch up with the war, I stopped and looked back at the field house where I had felt imprisoned and removed from reality. And that's when it hit me.

The reality of war doesn't just exist on the battlefield. It reaches out and touches everyone, everywhere. You cannot chase it and you cannot hide from it.

You can only hope it turns out like a basketball game, where the best team wins.

93

LAND, SEA, AIR

The Great Cooper River Bridge and Other Things Along the Way

In the early Saturday morning chill, to the beat of heavy metal music blasting from sidewalk speakers and the pounding feet of an army of would-be marathoners, I joined several thousand of my closest friends in the Great Cooper River Bridge Walk.

By doing so, I beat my personal best time of the year before by getting out of bed on time. For I had always thought the annual running and walking of the great span was a neat idea and a great photo opportunity for the sports pages, but just wasn't the kind of thing I was into early in the morning.

But I got my official Bridge Walk T-shirt and my official Bridge Walk number (5027) and waded into the throng of happy faces that clogged Mount Pleasant's Coleman Boulevard for the Great Walk. But first we had to wait for the Cooper River Bridge runners to flow through on their way to glory and infinite superiority—all 7,500 of them.

Like most people, I do not run often. The last time was when a slightly deranged man pulled a pistol on me while I was hitchhiking through New Jersey in the late '60s. But that's another story. For the most part I have not run without fear since I quit the high school track team.

For those who do, I honestly respect the passion you say you have for the sport and truly believe the stories you tell about the euphoric feeling you achieve from it. I did not, however, see any signs of such euphoria as I watched you head up the first span of the bridge. If that look on your face was euphoria, I'll settle for misery.

Anyway, after the runners shuffled by, the walking hordes converged on the streets, and this, my friends, is the true microcosm of Lowcountry America. People participating in the Great Cooper River Bridge Walk basically fall into three categories—old yuppies, young yuppies and others.

The first two categories are self-explanatory. The third category includes fat women, mothers pushing babies in strollers and merchant seamen who stumbled out of bars and got caught up in the crowd by mistake.

So off we went, our heads held high, the wind in our faces and our official Great Bridge Walk numbers flapping in the breeze. A great morning to be an American. A great day to be a Charlestonian. A bad day to be a tourist passing through town.

As we hit the first span of the old bridge, we were caught up in the pride of being a part of such a mass of humanity doing something good for ourselves and making a community statement about health and outdoor activity. Those who were not so enthusiastic about the Great Bridge Walk were the hundreds of motorists stranded on the new bridge where traffic had been stopped to let the happy mass of humanity pass.

But we did what all happy masses do on occasions like this—we waved to them and continued our quest. To the top of the bridge, inhaling the wonderful sights, sounds and smells of the river and marsh that we miss when we speed across the span in our cars each day. We were stopping to smell the roses. Decelerating the frantic pace of everyday life to become one with our surroundings and take notice of the little things we take for granted.

Like the condition of the old bridge. If this is a regular route for you the other 364 days of the year, I recommend you not look too closely at the old lady

when walking in the Great Cooper River Bridge Walk. The 50-year-old span looks a lot better when you can zip over it in about two minutes at 50 miles an hour.

But when you're trudging up the inclines, with your head lowered and your thighs wishing you'd stayed in bed, you become painfully aware of the cracks and corrosion and general shoddy condition it's in. Then you realize there are 20,000 overweight people packed on there with you and you pick up your pace and hope you make it to the other side before you become part of the Great Cooper River Bridge Collapse.

But you soon forget about that as you see the steeples of the Holy City on the horizon and realize you're padding downhill and heading for the home-stretch. And as you enter the Coca-Cola Hall of

Honor where the long-gone runners have scattered their water cups all over the road, the smiling faces of the East Side residents are strung along the corridor applauding your achievement.

Actually, they just came to be amused by a bunch of people who would pay $6 to walk across the Great Cooper River Bridge. But that's another story too.

And finally, more than an hour later, to the blaring music of "Chariots of Fire," good old number 5027 crossed the finish line at Marion Square and broke a world's record time, making it to the Portalets just in time.

And there the crowd grew larger as waves of walkers made their way into the sea of runners who

had been waiting all morning for us to arrive. It was not hard to distinguish who had run and who had walked.

The runners were the ones with the white official Cooper River Bridge Run numbers, the color coordinated running outfits and the confident smirks. The walkers were the ones with the purple official Cooper River Bridge Walk numbers, the really tacky outfits and the sore feet.

So there we gathered, the swift and the not-so-swift together in healthy harmony, soaking up the goodness of what we had done, bathing in the warm morning air, feeling great about being part of something so wonderful and wondering how we would get back across the Great Cooper River Bridge to where the car was parked.

Riding With That Damned Old Rodeo

Somewhere in the trail dust between romance and wrangling is rodeo. Ever since Buffalo Bill toured the world with his Wild West show, those of us who did not grow up on the backs of broncs and bucking horses have been fascinated with cowboys and the life they lead, or at least used to.

The rodeo, as presented at the North Charleston Coliseum, is a little old West mixed with modern-day entertainment. A recipe proven over the years.

A dash of dirt, a bit of flirtatious fringe, a teaspoon of terror, a hunk of horseflesh and a crowd in love with the idea is all you need.

Put all this to music and bring the house lights down, and you'd think you were in the wilds of Wyoming instead of the Lowcountry marshlands.

And if you dress right, shine up your boots and slide into some tight jeans that help tell your story, you too can be a part of the rodeo—at least for a little while.

Although rodeo is not a sport indigenous to South Carolina today, there is no doubt that there are cowboys among us.

All it takes is a big-hat mentality, a belt buckle the size of Dorchester County and a walk that says you've been on board and lived to tell about it.

In a very short time you're talking about the intricacies of bareback riding, the speed of steer wrestling, the grace of barrel racing and the all-out insanity of bull riding.

That's because there's a little cowboy in every one of us. That angry envy we felt as little boys when we realized we weren't born in Texas. That the only cowboys we'd probably ever know would ride up to our house on television. Or that we'd have to pack our six-guns to our hips and ride our imaginary stallions downtown to the picture show for our fix of heroics on horseback.

But alas, today most of us are only cowboys of the drugstore variety. More hat than horse. So we look with fixed fascination at the young boys standing around the corrals, tight in their britches, slim and stoic under their big, black hats. Always looking more comfortable with a horse than without one.

Or maybe that's why we all like something about rodeo. Because it's what we always thought we wanted to be, even though we knew in our hearts we never could.

But don't be fooled by the scenery. Rodeo today is big business, just like all the other professional sports.

The fresh-faced kids with their hats pulled down low are athletes all right. They've spent more time roping cows than most kids their age spend throwing baseballs. And where they come from, they are idolized like rock stars, as wildly as anyone who throws or catches a ball in this part of the world.

And they are professionals, riding and roping for big bucks on a big-time circuit most of us have never heard of. It is, however, the horse-and-cowboy version of NASCAR, complete with a point system and a national champion.

It's important stuff in their world, even though it never cracks the agate list in East Coast papers. Out west, where the cowboys live, it's the Super Bowl and March Madness all rolled into one.

But for most of us who did not move here from there, it's still a novelty.

Entertainment for the kids. Something different. A show that includes rope tricks and bull whips. Something to appreciate without having to know too much about it.

I think we all remember the first rodeo we ever saw. At least we remember how it smelled. That unmistakable mixture of sawdust, mud and manure. The scent of sweat steeped in saddle soap. The soft sweep of a cowgirl's hair in the wind.

That much, at least, hasn't changed.

The sport itself, however, has dug its spurs deep into corporate sponsorship for survival, and they are shameless hucksters when it comes to paying the bills.

But there is just enough danger and just enough clowning around to make it a world apart from our daily dosage of football and basketball. And if you close your eyes for a minute and let the myth of rodeo soak into your soul, you can still feel the legendary loneliness the cowboys sing about, and catch yourself riding with them when they come out of the chutes.

Riverfest: Celebrating the Edisto

With Brett Doolittle on the point and Beau Kennedy in the rear, our flotilla of canoes and kayaks turned slowly into the determined current of the Edisto River and headed downstream.

In upper Dorchester and Colleton counties, they are celebrating Riverfest, a human recognition of an ancient stream that now serves as a political boundary and common bond.

That's because rivers are things we don't use much any more. There was a time when they brought us what we needed and took away what we didn't. Their constant seaward motion has always been taken for granted, the way we expect the sun to rise and set, because it always has.

There was a time, however, when they served us well. In those long-ago days before super highways and airlines hubs, their meandering pathways were known by everyone who depended on their constant flow.

Now, we see them rarely, usually just a glance from the bridges as we speed overhead. A few bumps and they disappear in the distance.

But rivers like the Edisto are not forgotten by those who live near them, country folk who know where the fishing holes are, when they are rising, when they are falling, and what it all means.

As I guided a small kayak downstream, the real meaning was somewhere in the brown water that gurgled at the touch of the paddle.

Or somewhere along the wooded banks where willows bowed gracefully like large animals leaning down for a cool drink.

If there was another world out on the highways, it was soon forgotten on the river where the pace is set by gravity and nothing else.

On Saturday, as the Edisto took us along for the ride, courtesy of Carolina Heritage Outfitters, there was no other world for a few hours. To drift on the river is to forfeit control.

It has a mind of its own, and there is little you can do to change it.

Like most sports, this one is growing rapidly in popularity, mostly among people who have tired of keeping score.

On the river there is no clock. Time is kept by the millennium. What you see is what was there before and will be there when you leave.

And there is no scoreboard. Winners are those who crawl quietly out somewhere at the other end. Losers are the senseless spoilers of its pristine beauty and those who mistakenly think they own it.

For the most part, you are nothing more than a leaf or twig caught in the current. It is bigger and stronger than anything you can buy a ticket to ride, more powerful than anything you can hook onto the back of your boat.

You feel that, in fact, when you realize how far away you are from its beginning and end. That you are simply in the middle of its journey. That the force fueling your southward slide is almost invisible.

Because at times the river is so wide you seem to be sitting still, caught somehow in this chasm between trees and sky, locked in a motionless movement of things untamed.

But when it narrows and bends itself into a turn, there is no doubt of its downward determination. The ripples you hear around the bend are the only warning that its rush to the sea is on and you are part of it, like it or not.

There is no doubt that every person who has ever ridden a river comes away a little less sure of himself.

Even though we use them for sport of every kind, we hold no franchise on their comings and goings. We fish them and ride them and let our laughter drift out across them like smoke from our charcoal grills.

But we own no part of them, and they owe us nothing in return.

After a few precious hours on the back of the Edisto, we withdrew from its tug and hauled our boats to the shore, tired and weary, even though it had done all the work.

And in retrospect, you can only wonder if it ever knew we were there. For the water we rode was going along anyway. It was just kind enough to let us hitch a ride for a little while.

Adrift on the Lowcountry's Gentle Breeze

Just after dawn, as a morning fog hung close to the ground and the first glints of sunlight broke through the trees, Jim Eagle leaned out of the basket and kissed his wife goodbye.

Then with a few quick blasts of propane, the field below slipped away and we were airborne—softly, quietly and as gently as a feather caught in the early morning breeze.

Having flown on almost every kind of aircraft known to man, I was at first astonished at our rate of ascent, but even more taken by the silence.

Then as we drifted over the tops of a bordering pine thicket, the Lowcountry burst into view like a topographical canvas of colors and hues we seldom get to experience.

And as I watched Stono Ferry disappear behind us and the river marshes expanding below, I knew this was about as close to a birdlike experience as man is allowed to come.

Jim and his wife, Pam Eagle, operate Eagle Balloons almost as quietly as the large hot-air balloon itself.

They're in the phone book, but few know they're around unless they're lucky enough to see them drift quietly over their house some morning.

For me, this adventure was a birthday present from my wife, Ann, who had gone aloft during her reporting days in North Carolina.

And although I thought all my years of flying on military and commercial aircraft would prepare me for this, it was as close to a giddy experience as a man my age can come.

For all other flight had been a mixture of speed and power—man exercising his power over the air, dominating it with technology and jet engines.

Flights in my past had always had a mission, a destination, a time limit and a purpose.

But this was far removed from that. So far, in fact, that it hardly seemed like flight at all.

As our multicolored balloon appeared in the morning sky of John's Island, folks weighted to the ground by their daily routines stopped whatever they were doing to watch and wave.

Fisherman on the docks. Children waiting for school buses. People who normally ignore the constant passage of aircraft in our skies.

You can't help but look when a balloon passes overhead. You have no choice. Its pure simplicity commands your attention.

And the most amazing thing was that as you drifted over them, you could not only wave but talk to them.

"Fantastic," said one gentleman as he walked out on his back porch to view our passage. To which I had to agree.

From the brim of the basket I could see the Cooper River bridges in the distance, the subtle skyline of Charleston and the meanderings of the tidal rivers that make us what we are.

And down below, as we skimmed the treetops over long expanses of forests, deer would scamper through the brush as osprey circled us with distant curiosity.

In a world where control is often too important, ballooning is a chance to let yourself go on the wind.

Although we knew our direction when we lifted off, our final destination was as mysterious as an unsigned letter. West was our only flight plan.

Eventually, after soaking in the wonders of aimless navigation, Jim brought the big balloon to rest in a field far from where we departed. Pam soon found us in the chase truck and we packed the huge, deflated balloon into a trailer and were gone.

By this time the morning traffic was just beginning to build, as were the air currents we had used for our trip.

When I arrived in the office, people were milling around the newsroom as usual, having started their day on the ground where they would end it

But for me it was not just another day. It had started with a drifting ride in a hot-air balloon, and would end with a dream of silent, effortless flight.

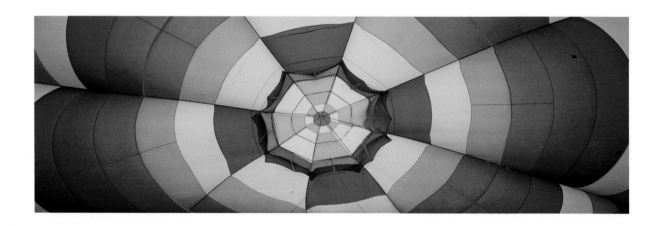

Charleston Boy at Home on the Harbor

There are, in reality, two Charlestons that are like fractured mirror images of each other, depending on where you are at any given moment. The one we are accustomed to is the one with narrow streets, horse-drawn carriages and tourists on every corner.

The other is the one that sits serenely in the harbor, its proud church steeples rising to the sky as beacons to cruise liners and ocean-going cargo ships. From the water, Charleston takes on the look of the port city it really is. A safe harbor for ships fresh off the vast expanse of the sea. A place of refuge and commerce and civility.

As Jack deftly maneuvered the small Widgeon through the light chop Sunday afternoon, a southwesterly breeze allowed us a tack against time as well as distance. A short trip that covered his 70-plus years as a Charleston boy at home on the water and the shore.

When he was young the city was much different. But when he was young, so was the world. Jack christened the small boat the Boo-Boo almost 30 years ago, and he has sailed it in regattas and on day trips with his three daughters, the youngest of whom is my wife, Annie.

Its original sails attest to the care and consideration he has given the vessel. The same attention to detail he has afforded his career as an architect, husband and father.

As I watched his weathered hand on the tiller, he talked of times when he was a boy and Mount Pleasant had a pristine beach where they would glide their crafts of the past up smartly to impress the girls. He courted and married one of them, Edith, and other than sailing the Pacific with the Navy in World War II, has spent his entire life not far from these shores.

So when he talks about changes, I listen. For in his words are the history of things nobody bothered to write down. The way the waters used to flow before deeper channels and progress closed creeks and forced the shrimp to school in different places. The

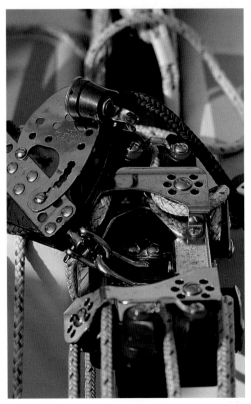